# Blinded By The White

## Volume 1
## Experiences on Confronting Racism

Forthcoming

*A Fish Doesn't Know It's Wet #MeTooARacist? (A Documentary)*
*Is White Supremacy a Mental Illness?*
*The America I Want to Live In Has Not Been Born Yet!*

# Blinded By The White

## Volume 1
## Experiences on Confronting Racism

# Jill A. Mesmer

Kansas City, Missouri
jillannmesmer@gmail.com



First Edition, 2021



Jill Mesmer
Blinded By The White
Volume 1
Experiences on Confronting Racism
Cover Photo: Jill Mesmer
Editor: Sara Henke
Editor and layout: Natasha Ria El-Scari www.natasharia.com
Cover design: Harold Smith  www.haroldsmith.com
Author photo: Kristy Blomquist

ISBN: 9798717937160

Printed in the United States of America

Dedicated to all members of white culture
willing to be introspective and a big shout of thanks to all
who have inspired this journey, you know who you are.

# TABLE OF CONTENTS

**ACKNOWLEDGMENTS**

I would be remiss if I took credit for the idea for this book series. One day my friend Harold Smith said, "Would you consider writing ten short essays about your experience recognizing your white privilege? I will help you publish."

In the four years I have been immersing myself in this racism journey, when I listen to these "suggestions" as if they were a "divine download," there are miracles and healing that happen each and every time.

We need to learn how to really listen to each other for the healing of the great divide we are currently experiencing in this nation.

My sincere intention is that these and subsequent experiences and essays will help facilitate that!

**NOTE TO THE READER**

Realizing I won the skin lottery resulting in White privilege was abhorrent to me. I did nothing to earn it. It comes at the expense of all others. I will use White privilege to amplify voices not heard.

I thank you in advance for your ongoing interest in upcoming volumes, the documentary and my art. Not everyone can march, but all can contribute by supporting this work until all necessary changes are a reality.

## FOREWORD

It is one thing to research African American history not taught in public schools. In fact, every White person seriously needs to do just that...STAT! It begs the question why is "our" history mandatory but "Black History" is elective?

But recognizing both the big picture and everyday areas where White privilege has escaped our notice is also VITAL. It helps to look at life beyond our White lenses to see where we might adjust our thinking and actions.
It is up to the "privileged" to correct the system that oppresses others while we continuously benefit.

If you claim to love this country, then let us unite to make the necessary changes so "Liberty and Justice for All" is LITERALLY true for the first time in American history! And we will go down on the right side of history promoting equity and equality in an unprecedented way. The slow roll of gradualism is OVER! Here is a "fun fact," if your life does not flash before you because death is a serious possibility when a policeman/woman pulls you over, congratulations...you have White privilege!

So, let us be very clear...White privilege does not mean your life has not been hard. It simply means it has not been hard due to your skin color.

Artwork By: Alexis Mesmer Rebman

# #1. Genealogy While White!

When I began my internal inquiry about racism, I pointed to my mother's ancestor William Herndon as a positive example. He was Abraham Lincoln's law partner and sided with Lincoln on the issue of slavery. His father Archer Herndon who served in the Illinois state legislature with Mr. Lincoln, but he was sympathetic to the slave owners. It was a house divided like my family of origin today. But my thought at the time was, well at least I do not have to apologize for relatives who owned slaves. Upon further inquiry, there **were** relatives out in West Virginia that did own slaves. Of course I am hearing that they were such a benevolent slave owner that when the slaves were offered their freedom, they stayed because conditions were so good. Eye roll!  I can only hope that was the case, but my gut tells me it is an attempt to justify this hideous practice.

So, I wrote an essay four years ago about waking up to racism and how the above internal dialogue along with many other inquiries was instrumental.

"A Fish Does Not Know It's Wet #MeTooARacist?" is the title of my documentary.

 Since I was estranged from my own family, knowing who they all were was really of minimal interest to me. But as I came to appreciate the African American experience, it seemed like many were orphans with no hope of ever finding birth parents or relatives. Walking a mile in their shoes, I must admit that would truly haunt me. And then to watch those of the slave owner/oppressor class, aka White people, be able to research their ancestry with ease would just rub salt in the wound. I had zero appreciation for this privilege and understand the disgust some might have had toward me because of this privilege. My attitude was, "Some of my relatives weren't such great human beings while they were here. They would probably sabotage me from the other side." But no, the melanated part of my tribe patiently taught me the value of our ancestors' energy and help from the other side. "Your ancestors' prayers are still protecting you." This in turn sparked a journey of forgiveness with both deceased parents which has the ultimate gift of freedom called inner peace. Emancipation initiated by BLACK folks. Oh, the irony!

They owed me exactly **nothing**, yet this gift is **everything!**

Photo by: Jan Mesmer Fowler

# #2. Vaping While White

A girlfriend and I were in the parking lot of a drinking establishment at about dusk when parking lot security came rolling through. I remember in my younger years when I would be a magnet for suspicion with my paranoid behavior. My friend looked over at me and said, "Don't act all hinky, this is where we just thank our White privilege and wait for them to pass." No spoiler alerts, that is exactly how it went down. Had we been Black, it may have been a whole different experience. At the very least, more than likely they would have been asked what they were doing there and to show an ID. The rest would have been up to the sum of the experiences of the security guard about race. We have seen repeatedly the worst-case scenarios of this and all points in between. We did converse about what it will feel like to always have a target on your back especially if you get in the wrong crosshairs. Both of us being survivors of sexual abuse could relate somewhat to the idea of being a target. Fight, flight, or freeze is the bodily reaction, and it is hell on the parasympathetic nervous system. Science has shown it is responsible for a host of ailments, disorders, and diseases. Little wonder the COVID-19 pandemic hit this and other communities of color so disproportionately hard.

Photo by: Jill Mesmer (selfie)

# #3. Walking While White

Maybe you have heard of driving while Black, walking while Black? Well, this is not that!

While recovering from narcissistic abuse and simultaneously learning about racism, I would take refuge at a gorgeous, wooded park near my home. Dusk and dawn were my magical, favorite times because with the changing of the guard so to speak, different wildlife would appear. I must admit, there were times when I was so lost in my experience I stayed way later than what would have been deemed safe. Pictures were posted to social media and many of my women friends would express concern. I was gifted a couple of tasers which pacified some. But my Black women friends were not as easily convinced. Finally, it was brought to my attention that women of color whether Native American, Black, Latino, etc. go missing every day, but mainstream America does not know or report this. Tell me again how "All lives matter?" They had true concerns for my safety, but I labeled it paranoia because I could not take in the love behind it. I did finally connect the dots...it was a privilege to feel like I could walk where they dare not tread alone. With the added layer that if I were assaulted, I would have a better chance of being believed than any woman of color. And we all know that is a slippery slope even for white women.

To say that I value my Black women friends is an understatement! Some are truly a sister from a different mister.

Photo by: Jill Mesmer, Line Creek, Kansas City, MO

## #4. Shopping While White

It was a little further into my inquiry about racism when I was walking in a department store. I usually leave my big purse in the car since all of that does not fit in the wristlet that I use while shopping. So here I was, walking through the store with prescription sunglasses on, identity obscured, yet completely unbothered by any store clerks or loss prevention officers. When I realized how privileged that looked, I took them off and only used them when I needed to see something sharply. I was pretty stunned by my new revelation. Ever see the signs that say no hoodies, sunglasses, or backpacks? Three guesses as to who that is targeting. Do you experience being followed, detained, or searched when you shop? Me neither.

The clerk who rang me up was a very sweet, petite Black woman. I felt compelled to say, "These are prescription sunglasses, I left my glasses in the car. I understand how privileged this might look." She was very gracious and said, "thank you, that means a lot." Owning my privilege does not fix anything. That is what the ballot box is for.

But owning it lets the other person know that at least I am aware and working on it.

Photo by: Teresa Goodman of Harvest Moon Botanica

## #5. Driving While White

Last fall, a friend and I went to view the autumn colors out east and pick up a car they had found online in Cleveland.

I was following them back home making sure I kept proper distance. If you have ever been rear ended, you become hyper aware of this. So, we are sitting at a stoplight and I hear screeching tires behind me. One glance in the rearview mirror and I said audibly "not a-fucking-gain" as I braced for impact. BAM! It was the second time being rear ended in two years. Thankfully, I did not hit my friend's new car.

We each pulled around the corner to get off the busy road but the woman that hit me went straight. Thankfully, she pulled over into another parking lot and did not try to run. The police that she had already called passed me as we were both trying to get to her. When the officer was going to take my statement, I said that I felt we all needed masks. She looked mildly irritated but put hers on. I was faced with a dilemma...

I had a choice of putting on a generic black paper mask or my Black Lives Matter mask. It felt like complete failure as an ally because I chose the paper mask. I did not want to enflame the officer considering the protests still rightfully going strong from the murder of George Floyd. A dead, jailed, or hospitalized ally is no benefit to anyone. I had a choice, but people cannot change the color of their skin when they might be in danger. It seriously haunted me, so I discussed it with a Black friend when I got home. She was like, "Are you crazy?"

Me: "...Well yes."

Her: "We would do the same thing in your shoes. All we ask is that you own your privilege!" She also said at a different time, "The best thing White people can do is say, 'Yes I'm White, yes I'm privileged, I have implicit bias, but I want to learn and be your friend.'" White culture is very passive aggressive by nature, but this direct approach is necessary.

If I had to watch a group of people enjoying privilege, completely oblivious to that fact, I would find it nauseating. And some do, yet the African American friends in my life continue to show grace, mercy, and forgiveness repeatedly. They are not interested in retaliation; they just want the 400+ yrs. of oppression to cease. That is precisely where those of us who are privileged have the responsibility of fixing the system that continues to oppress them, while consistently elevating us for centuries.

Photo by: Jill Mesmer (selfie)

# #6. Sitting While White

After the incident with "central park Karen" last summer in New York City, I was sitting on my friend's front step waiting for her to come out due to COVID-19. I remember thinking, I am so glad this neighborhood is used to my car and my face being here. I felt slightly unsafe for the first time EVER in three years being in her neighborhood. When she came out, I revealed what I had been thinking. I remember her kind of rolling her eyes and saying, "you just don't get it, yet do you?   White folks can move around in any public space without raising an eyebrow because it is a White man's world. Nobody here is going to mess with you unless you start acting a fool. It's not all about you." Again, I love her directness in stark contrast to White culture which is extremely passive aggressive.

That obvious fact had escaped my notice and the only time I felt unsafe was in my own head due to misinformation. Both from the way Black people are misrepresented in the media as something to fear (criminals, drug addicts, thugs, etc.), and my resulting socially conditioned misconceptions. It deeply saddens me each time layers of this privilege are revealed. How could I have been so blind for almost six decades?   It quickly turns to activism in wanting to close the gap, so **all**  have equal privilege in life. I realize this is a Mount Everest climb, but we must start **and** finish no matter the obstacles. White people standing in solidarity with minorities voting to change the racist layers designed into the system is at critical mass. Also, one of the worst, most threatening alliances for the Powers that be. White supremacy which is social conditioning taken to extreme, could possibly result in mental illness. This is what we are up against, but it is imperative that we truly unite. We recently witnessed the reality of this united success first-hand in Georgia's elections in 2020.

# #7. Waking Up While White

Over a decade ago, there was a powerhouse Black woman from Center for Spiritual Living who held a law degree and is a successful playwright. She was also hilarious, so I just had to meet her for coffee. She was honestly the one that got me wondering how she, as a Black person, overcame the odds against her and was so accomplished as a result. That winning formula had escaped me for five decades, so I listened, watched, and observed basically on Facebook. Her information about racism came so fast and furiously that I had to "unfollow" her for my sanity's sake. At least that was my perception at the time.

Wow let us just unpack that for a minute. Her truth about my oppressive race and what it did to Black people was non life-threatening to me, so I get to leisurely wake up at my own pace since my very life did not depend on it? Holy run-on sentence Batman! If that is not the zenith of White privilege, please inform me as to what it is?

It appears minorities need to remain hyper vigilant to have a prayer of successfully navigating the land mine called the White man's world. What if their energy expended just to survive could be channeled in partnership with willing White folks to create a better world for all?

I for one would like to test this theory, so who else is in? Look what Stacy Abrams accomplished with a team of equals! I rest my case.

# #8 Traveling Abroad While White

Before everything hit the fan in 2020, I traveled with a friend to Kenya and Uganda to scratch off my number one bucket list item...a photo safari. That, in and of itself ,is privilege. They say humans originated from Africa, but I do not have any quantifiable roots there. Some who do will never get there, because racism in America is about keeping the Black population subjugated, especially through inequity and economic disparity.

Nangabo Bright Junior School, Kampala Uganda
Photo by: Dennis Dehn

I had not connected the dots as to how much of a target I was going to be with this White face. It was synonymous with money to young and old alike. With Uganda being a police state at the time, you could be pulled over by someone in uniform and must pay a bribe to proceed. Our host and friend paid the first bribe while in Kampala. The second time we were at Entebbe airport when our friend informed the officer that we were his friends and appearances were deceiving.  My great big $5.00 thrift store watch suggested wealth. No bribe paid, but the corruption was rampant with seemingly nowhere to turn for justice.

It got to where if I would see someone in uniform while riding, I would get very busy with something on the floor and just avoid the situation. And let me be very clear...
The trip was wonderful in so many other ways. I am just making a point here.

In Kenya it was more of being a target to buy things and spend money in Nairobi rather than chain of command corruption. The safaris were a nice respite for that and so many other reasons. But after a couple of weeks of being a target, I managed to be the only White person at the Nairobi airport when leaving. Then they put me on the wrong flight, so I had to be called by name and parade out to go get re-processed and on a different flight. I have never felt more self-conscious and conspicuous in my life.

So, a few of my takeaways from that experience were, every White person should have to feel what I experienced. Being a target for the color of your skin with no assurance of justice is a completely helpless feeling. I found myself hyper alert for anything in uniform so I could take precautions. My anxiety was off the chart. But the difference is, I could come back to America where I am second on the food chain only to the White male. Blacks in America cannot escape being a target for racism unless and until White folks acknowledge their privilege and vote to truly equalize our system, not just pacify with platitudes, and promises.

# #9 Motives While White

Have you ever said or done something with what you thought was a pure motive and been completely blindsided by the other person's reaction?

That has happened too many times to count on this journey so I will give you just a few highlights. It is part of the process of unlearning layers and layers of conditioning.

There is an African philosophy called Ubuntu that basically states, "I am because we are." Inclusivity and community are the building blocks for a successful society and the six letters would fit perfectly on my license plate. It would spark conversation about race, and I would be able to use it to be an "ally." Pure motive, right? So, I posted on social media about wanting this on vanity plates. I thought the motive made it OK! Boy was I wrong! What was missing was a clear understanding of cultural appropriation versus cultural appreciation. Being the dominant culture, this UBUNTU could get swallowed up in whiteness and lose its originality. White culture has appropriated, stolen, and erased accomplishments of Black culture for centuries. Remember the movie Hidden Figures? The buck stops here!

Because we have enjoyed privilege for centuries, it takes humility to be corrected by, and learn from, those you may have subconsciously been taught to feel "better than." When I adopted the view that I needed to listen as if the Divine were channeling through them, "magic and miracles" became a regular thing in my life. My documentary will expound on this.

This next example would come under the heading of "refinement" for me. I made a comment on social media about an up-and-coming gymnast who was breaking all sorts of records. My comment was, "Move over Simone Biles, she's coming for you!" In my mind, I envisioned Simone Biles being the inspiration for this other gymnast to the point where they joined forces on the same Olympic team. What on earth could be wrong with that? That was the motivation for the comment.

Again, one of my friends pointed out that Black folks are severely underrepresented in the gymnastic world. The comment appeared to pit these two athletes against each other and cause further division, the very last thing this community needs. So, let me be very clear...my motive was irrelevant! I needed to look at this through something other than my White lenses. What matters is how it lands on the listener. This kind of refinement can feel to White folks like the fulfillment of what I was taught, "they complain about everything and appreciate nothing given to them." I unpack this statement in the documentary.  Suffice it to say, we need to actively listen when we are told how our words, thinking and actions affect others, especially communities of color if we truly want to resolve these issues.

Photo by: Jill Mesmer, Line Creek Park, Kansas City, MO

# #10 Being Liberal While White

Up until about four years ago, I would not even entertain the idea of being racist because I was a Liberal! I did not view the poor, immigrants, people of color etc., as the problem so I was for equality. Boy was I in for quite an awakening when George Floyd was murdered while the whole world watched. For the record, it was only a few short years ago that I would have been posting the same thing. So, I feel that I can speak with experience and authority about this. Certainly not in a position to judge. I saw a post from liberal White folks weighing in on things like:

How the Black community grieves their losses! I saw posts by White Liberals saying that "George Floyd was almost attaining sainthood by the Black community. And when you look at his criminal record, he should not be revered at all. He committed violence against women among many other things and while he didn't deserve to die, he doesn't need to be worshiped either." The beginning and the end of this discussion is basically, we are so used to white privilege we feel our opinions/voice need to be heard on every given subject. How could we possibly know what it is like to live in Black skin in America? The sheer hubris.

Or the comments by Liberals about Black Lives Matter not using the phrase, "defund the police." Again, never having been on the other end of racial profiling or police brutality, the sheer hubris of thinking that we know what is best and everyone needs to know our brilliant ideas. Where is the follow-through for change? Liberals have failed the Black community in ways different than Conservatives.  But make no mistake, both have failed, or we would be in a different place today. Check out the documentary "Crack…Cocaine, Corruption and Conspiracy" if you doubt the validity of my statement.

Art work by: Adrianne D. Clayton

I also had a friend come to me wanting me to resolve a debate between her and her daughter relating to race. I have to say I was truly honored that her opinion of me was one of knowledge and fairness on this subject.  My friend felt like rap music and artists were not doing their community any favors with their lyrics using the N-word and violence against women. Her daughter was saying it was not her issue to expound on. I am friends with a 76-year-old sharecropper's daughter who happens to agree with my White friend about rappers and the content they feed their listeners. Only one of these two women have the right to espouse an opinion about this subject. Any guesses?

This experience, barely preceding George Floyd's death, sparked a journey for my friend to explore racism with a fervor I have never seen before. She put me to shame with her studious inquiries and applying it in her thinking and in her life. More of this please.  She was and continues to be incredibly inspiring. I must believe there are many more like her who are ready for positive change.

My sincere and heartfelt desire is that more White folks will be inspired to take the introspective journey and help "be the change" we want to see in the world. We are at critical mass with two possible outcomes as Dr. Martin Luther King Jr. states, "We must learn to live together as brothers or perish together as fools."

# ABOUT THE AUTHOR

Jill Mesmer lives in Kansas City, MO which is where she began her anti-racist journey. She hopes to be fully retired from her cleaning business as soon as possible. When she isn't upsetting her fellow white people she enjoys live music, theatre, creating activism art and traveling.

www.ingramcontent.com/pod-product-compliance
Lightning Source LLC
Chambersburg PA
CBHW070228260726
48658CB00006BA/2215